Stories That Listen

Also by Priscilla Becker

Internal West

Stories That Listen

Priscilla Becker

Four Way Books
Tribeca

Please direct all inquiries to:
Editorial Office
Four Way Books
POB 535, Village Station
New York, NY 10014
www.fourwaybooks.com

Library of Congress Cataloging-in-Publication Data

Becker, Priscilla, 1965-
Stories That Listen / Priscilla Becker.
p. cm.
ISBN 978-1-935536-05-5 (pbk. : acid-free paper)
I. Title.
PS3602.E29S76 2010
811'.6--dc22

2010001564

This book is manufactured in the United States of America and printed on acid-free paper.

Four Way Books is a not-for-profit literary press. We are grateful for the assistance we receive from individual donors, public arts agencies, and private foundations.

This publication is made possible with public funds from the National Endowment for the Arts

and from the New York State Council on the Arts, a state agency.

Distributed by University Press of New England
One Court Street, Lebanon, NH 03766

We are a proud member of the Council of Literary Magazines and Presses.

This book is dedicated to the life and memory of Alexandra Rudnitsky

"... I would
link the minutes of my days close, somehow, to your days."
—Muriel Rukeyser

Table of Contents

○

O

White Tone

I think I prefer now being unloved
and listening for my footsteps in the dark.

There was a tree in the yard—
not any more—
whose crooked branch I'd watch.

I held a ceremony in which I married
my black dog.

There is a certain smell
that overtakes me, for instance
once, in a button shop.

And then I came to disregard.

Also a kind of nakedness
that has to do with words.

I made a list
of things I'd like. I tied
a string. The sound as when your foot
breaks through the snow,
that sound was in the house.

The Inner Life

Something had been left
sketched, incomplete—a thinness
wearing into transparency,
nubile and ancient,
the hole that one is
and falls into.

But there were intimations—
getting lost in a library,
emerging after dark, feeling
as though you had eaten,
had lived for a time in a fitted
skin—held and correct—
like an animal, without thought.

No wonder where the day had gone.

You heard a voice,
the correct sort of fear
like crossing a line out,
walking away from home,
the kind of time cannot
be counted—swathed
head, shut mind, something
alive in a tomb.

Morning as an archaeologist,
a feeling like restoration—
bringing out original
intent, the shape you made
before words

No clothes—
naked, prostrate, without
ordering, a fully furnished
round thing with all the things
you like to see and say and
touch and think and feel and
hear—a complete
picture of these things.

Hypnosis

I think last summer you said the word
in almost life-long drawn-out time,
perfected the gesture with your hand
you'd started prehistorically that snapped me
back, as though we had agreed.

And all the times that I was high, not
the exceptions they seemed to be
but regular rhythms, etherized.

Perhaps I should more patiently describe
the snapping's familial lingering—as there was
nothing quick or precise; it more reminded me
of a glacier I read patronized in a book
    of geologic phenomena.

Because if you were standing close,
at the fortuitous time, you would hear
the generational crack of coldness breaking
free, and see the separate chiseled
    facets gliding by.

Blue Statuary

The songs wore out; they rusted
the radio. The singers began to die.
I left my toenails at the beach, hoping
they would grow another body.
I would return with a better,
more expressive face.

I loved it when you said my name.
When you didn't, I listened
to the sounds the world made.
The trees especially injured me,
though they wouldn't have known.
When the wind arrives, it upsets them.

I would return with sand in my hair.
The silence, I expected.

Euthanasia

This canopy, an eyelet sky, a white that's called
in certain circles, for instance the one that binds
the four posts of the bed, *old*
bride, is sipping-slow.

The statue on the lawn, carved
saint·the veins inscribe   I wait
patient as a stone, compliantly
erode, for you to put me there.

I want it plain. I want
the North or far South Pole,
and all the mid-Atlantic states,
the room and its room-
temperature, to take their leave
    and go.

The view emits its endless season.
But somehow gladder sufferers are gliding
toward the world of glass, the cactus bed,
    where I first read
    how it should be done.

I cannot think of any reason
the sheet's well-meaning mothering
should not like other motherings go awry
and twist its skirts and nurse me backwards—
    acute, local, kind:

Reverse this slipping mouth-
to-mouth. I am not linked to any
current.

afters

at long last the feeling
like a night with some
stars, a day with the keys
home left home
as though you'd been
    a mime

you don't recognize
everything clean
but the part of you that builds
and accumulates has been
erased and you can start
over, not over but
before, not before but
with ugly knowing

you've moved across
the red grey landscape
and you can act now
partly innocent of yourself

Hatred of Men with Blond Eyebrows

It was not without omen—
the owl at the back
of the lecture hall, the dream
of old men in white bathing caps.

    But I was arrogant
    about that.

The doorway seemed a momentary
place, but soon I made a nest—
pink styrofoam, calipers, rubber bands,
siroccos of fur

I think I'd be judged if I left.
But there's a deception I know:
the body can move on its own.

Math Poem

Because it will not snow
we calculate in inches
our quietism.

The whiteness of our eyes diminishes
as from the year's prophetic
poison, our long drag finishes.

I found it democratic
leaving sloughings of ourselves
in every coffee shop, pseudo-

scientific. The tally under-
whelms. But still I collect
specimen, I line the shelves.

The virtual calendar subtracts.
Examining my maps: no sex
till Nova Scotia I predict.

Each year about this time I resurrect
my vows to vultures, cults,
the obliterative X.

Sedentary Sea Organisms, Mostly Algae

Figure number six deceived me—
the nubs and false handles,
like concrete poured unevenly,

though I have seen a device
for keeping necklaces—itself an ornament—
like a golden cactus, and thought I saw
myself.

And it was at a party, or I should say,
a room of voices and colors, the room
I had walked out of, that I felt the pull
of family.

And when I touched it, as I never should,
some of the threads caught in my sleeve.
And I thought of the sculpture—
the only one I know—of the woman
reclining, her ankles touching.

And I heard the awful mix of voices
and music pushed out of songs and
plates and glasses and the one voice always
louder than the others.

And at night I had a dream and I
remembered it: I walked into the water.
And the gentle and obscene sound
of water, and the obscene smell.

Logic

It was a mistake to have loved you.
It is not bitterness that causes me
to say so but logic—a consolation
of the heartbroken, one of the last
    to show.

It is a mistake to call logic
cold; it has no temperature at all.
It merely reveals itself
when the last of the emotion
    is gone.

It was there all along.
Now your face is like a face,
nothing more. It reminds me
of a fact—not a particular one.

I see you through a bodiless
faculty, as a stone might see
its mineral cause. It is not
an emotion, it is a thought.

Still Life Without Drugs

Only white and the music
of the institutionalized
Maybe the artist
is satisfied
If you look long enough
you will begin to see

hallucination's opposite—
domesticity—the landscape
lining up like a list

Your outside edge is also
the edge of air: put
your finger there, study
your own hand

Soon you will begin
to fill the page
with your dead hope,
the paraphernalia of
the glib-faced young—
blown dandelion skin,
clenched head

In the afterlife
(you'd like to come back
as a gnat, something
with the power to distract)
every shadow, collapsed

vein, false vampire, burned
word becomes available
Only you could make
such color look like
so much emptiness

Numberless Hand Series

I thought of a paralysis
a stiffening of the ligaments
so that the hand looked
in a shock. At first I only
mourned the loss of curl
around my coffee cup, the warmth
   within my palm.

But soon I thought of other
horror, and also of the way that it
occurs—in increments, a segment
   here or there.
I've never seen it whole.

A Minor Language

Finally I have begun to die.
No blood or missing words
informed me, no resurged
affection for earth; I have no
sudden connecting need or
attraction to higher anythings.

But recently (and this is
part of it: time has become
indistinct to me) I met
an aspect of the natural world,
a genus unknown to me.

I think if I were to take you there
you might not necessarily see
the particular quality—

It was a flower, flower-
color, standing where
it was supposed to be—
in a row of planted things,
its idle face surveying
the scene indifferently.

Oh I have seen more
beautiful things, I've
observed more unusual
occurrences; I'm not clairvoyant
and I have no special hearing.
That is not the point I'm making:
this flower did not speak
(though if it did it would
have had nothing to say about unity).

It's just the kind of thing
one notices—
after the extremes—
a kind of sobriety
that must mean,
because it has no
meaning to anyone but me,
that I have begun
to believe such things.

Midwestern

After what was likely half
my life I began to understand
what was required:

abstinence from mood, refusal
of the bundled nerves.

Therefore when all the clichés
gather in the bars at noon
you find yourself a professional
distance away

And is that why machine-age
artifacts spread like wildfires
in the west—the sound

of hammering, metals
pressed flat

On almost every corner
there's a version of the song
—sour twang,
reworked words

Therefore you find yourself
in lessened light, walking off
the afternoon.

Communication by the Remnants of Fire

When I got your note with the little
exploded plant fibers inside, in the muted
camouflage of the vegetable kingdom
and the smell of the swamp, but also
of your Chanel face powder that you sold
your employer's books on the side for a month to buy,
the yellowed blotches on the paper
and the brown spot that framed
a transparency, made a collage.

The envelope sounded very old,
like the dryness just before disintegrating,
or the scratching wings of insects in trees,
and there was a fragment of a yellow print
obscuring your words which had been smudged
by a fraction of an ounce of Chanel Mademoiselle.
I tried to scrape together enough dust
to fill a bowl or roll a minuscule cigarette.
I thought perhaps that this was your intent.

Reconstruction

October, light belonging
to simpler, longer time,
a desperate humidity,
confused green, I took a tour
of your former apartments.

The yellow one affected
me most; I moved among
the satellite establishments,
infused with future

Its ribbed garish shingles
had stopped offending, the greasy
acrylic smell. It was now a place
of sad pornography, like the South.

I think I was waiting for you,
at the corner, like I used to.

A prurience for the way we
used to be, for all our old
feelings new.

Psalm for No One

Dear ________,
It is now that I need you

I hope my voice can
bring you near

It is hard to picture
no one so I think of the girl
    who died

her bright face, the way
she says yes to everything

There shouldn't be in a bed
more pillows than heads

You shouldn't dream
of the person beside you

Please call down rain,
a storm to carry away
our former homes

We will open our mouths
and wash out
remembrance of ourselves

Dear ________,
forgive me for not
standing among stars

I make no sacrifices—
though there has been blood

And I am not faithful—
though there have been times
when something followed me home

The girl, does she see everything
Do flakes of her fall with the snow?

Please let there be
times when I am forgetting

like the smell of marigold

Also I don't worship anything
except for once I knelt
at the back of the bar

How will I know if you've heard me

________ *of no echo*
________ *of shallow halls*

I am not superstitious
________ *of empty rivers*

I have no talent for awe

Monksbane

When I couldn't find the season
stranger, I imagined you as winter.

And in your gesture, the tentative
snow, I located your wish to remain

mysterious to yourself. I tried to walk
the blank boughs, concerned,

though that is my term, with the narrow
passageways that branch beneath my feet.

Because that seemed to be the nature,
though it is just my word, from which
    the form is released.

Recurrence of Childhood Paralysis

The dog lay dead in the backyard for days
and I sacrificed a doll to keep
him company in the earth.

The mulberry trees, which I have mentioned,
dropped hot fruit.

That nostalgia followed me,
a negligent strain—imprecise and unhappy.

The ground is sere
as though a jar had covered it.

A little like a lazy eye, I'd been
not precisely where I seemed.

I hope you are imagining my childhood.

Like sleeping, it was once described to me,
but knowing that you sleep. Once I wanted
very much to say I love you—that,
but bodily.

On Being Left For No One

Thursday will be cold. You
imagine a man walking
the coast—windmill, salt,
and across the water, fire.

But he is not a romantic man
though his face turns to profile.
And before he left it was like
    paper
                    with a graph.

And the coast is just some
place you conjure because
there are so many hours in a day—
Can you live on it: wet
light, shells, the many waves
they must roll under

And before he left it was like
    shirts, white
                    with starch.

From your shallow space
you contemplate the attraction
of the coast, the line
between two things,
choosing nothing:

There is no argument for yourself.

Simulation

Sometimes
when it's been gone
so long

like winter's infinity
or an everlasting sleeper car

When 10:01 has come
and gone

a cloud of former
nature floats by

It's like being
unemployed

Mountains of purpose
assemble close

Once there was something
to erect

a minuscule monument
un-analyzed

Once there was something
to drag out

Then it was like
increments that won't
collect

an occasional bout
of coincidence

Once it was possible
to idolize

Then it was like
artifacts receding
from a vault

a waiting
place, nothing
to describe

Moving Images

Were it night, the sound of the crow—
high, complaining—would seem a sound
    striking out alone

uncrowded by electric locusts' chattering,
unsurrounded by the courtyard baby assembly.

Its freedom is what troubles me,
the borderless quality of its cry, a sound
that in the day seems part of a scene
and one could see the black body
    heaving by.

But at night the sound divests itself,
like those other awful independent
sounds—the clanging gate, the rusted swing—
that make me picture the scene just before
    their happening.

Leaving Song

There is a sound that something
makes when it is leaving—
not lonesome, not arrogant—
though the leaving I am thinking
about isn't sneaking out.

But rather a kind of pacing
that's taken on direction, a sound
of purpose, a long stride
which neither ambles nor
    runs out.

Like slow rain
that starts a few towns over

A sound for already-
stunted figures, pulled up
from back wards of imagination
that tells you *something's*
set in motion, something
somewhere's been set free.

Monarch

Your rule has made an August
of October and I am lazy
in my domicile as maple leaves
turn half yellow and forget
the ailing spectrum.

This season there are many
kings; I've made a shrine
to orange things, a coterie
of me and three domestic-
leaning cats whose naps fulfill
a mossy genuflection brought on
by molding walls, delays
in evolution.

I thought I saw you drinking from
a branch between the pickets
of a fence, and in two gestures
you define first aviation,
then verticality. And as I wait

for long-diverted patterns, triumphal
browns, the cat's serene totem
of itself says there's a lineage
denied me. Still I would like to rule
a small bud too, but I have neither
your erect and glassy wings nor

did I come from emerald shroud:
I drink the milk of thistle, preferring
it to natural motherings.

Words Above a Poem

If I tell another
language, watch its
blonde eyebrows quake, its
impassive face

My simple phrases, rudimentary
hands pointing away
You will think
I can be fooled

I chose a mountain
place. Mineral cures, mine
baths, vapor caves.
I speak in fog

Corner & Square

One summer I wrote you more
letters than you deserved. Among
friends I burned with all the curse-
words I would say. I could not wait
to get back home, to speak to you
in silent tones for all the nights
which did not speak a word to you.

I often now have little to say,
and sounds I could not say I hear.
I avoid the center of the room;
I like the table's edge, any sharp
place; the dull surface is a friend.
I sometimes do not go, I stay.

I am like the mountain: you can mark
the time of day across my face.

Natural Cause

When we were young we liked
to pick the way we'd die—you
trapped in a fire and the next-door-
neighbor boy crushed in a mining
disaster; our slow Canadian cousin
struck down in a rush of bullets
following his pursuit for weeks
because he'd done something unlawful.

And we liked to speak for others too,
deciding our parents would be swept
away on an antediluvian wave, our dolls,
over a slow and painful course,
succumb to button and stuffing loss.

And I said I would like to die of remorse.
I pictured my body as a house.
As in a dream each door I pushed
seemed not to recognize my touch.

Dr Hegy's Magic Table

At four o'clock I wished
that it was over

but it was the brown one that came
so easily to my hand.

Asphyxiated by my own
ammonia, I would launch
the contact, and from the other side
respond.

I remember opening the cage.
The bird hopped to the center.

When did you die?

Blackness squandered in the trees,
the table broken, crest
of the bird high.

It must have been my fingers
that pushed the planchette to spell out
words that were never there.

The letters tilted to one side,
sinking into the table formed by our fingers.

When will it be September?

Last in Water Series

When it is time, I will choose
the most beautiful river.
I compare swatches cut
from maps, samples drawn
from the world's waters.

It's been a while since
I was surrounded in element,
some time since
the blue mothering.

I am aware of the marble-
patterned floor—dizzying
but not warm.

It is a mutual need,
and even when I am doing
the most obscure thing,
I sense the water
moving toward me.

I smell the river's brine
as though it's the water
    inside me.

I'd like for my river
to be visited infrequently,
for the sediment to be high.

The sound it will make,
a calling.
Not my name
but my name
before there was speech.

Retraction of Vow

It's easier now, removed
from the temporary

scaffolding of your bones

besides, there was something
unreliable and I never walked

entirely below. It is an average day,

perhaps a birthday of someone
neither young nor old

On Nothing

The other morning we awoke
from nothing—a night had passed,
an existential night with no boundary—
a dark continuing of day.

From nothing, a night had passed
into deeper nothing, our dreams
a dark continuation of day
so that everything appeared the same.

Into deeper nothing our dreams
climbed backwards, blacker
so that everything appeared the same.
Our bodies, sexed into twin regimen,

climbed backwards, blacker
(not a flying dream but a walking one).
Our bodies sexed into twin regimen
walking beside each other, walking slow

Not a flying dream but a walking one
(it could take a long time for it to be over);
walking beside each other, walking slow,
we had begun to dream about home.

It could take a long time for it to be over
(the existential night with no boundary):
walking beside each other, walking slow,
the other morning we awoke.

Part of Water Series

1.

I don't think I ever thought
when I walked to the lake
and looked across the water to the other
side, my bed sheet wound in my arms,
and the buildings looming farther
and farther behind, and the things
I always bring—I don't know
what (precisely) they are—banging
my hip rhythmically, and the clothes
I wear obsessively (I have been told
the key to warmth is layering)

I mean I don't think I recognized
that a person walking at my side
might turn at any moment a severe
degree and that it might be done
with very little thought for me

I like to think of smoke and how it
dares not make a sound but lends
a color to the air and an exacting smell,
and how impossible it is to tell
if it is even really there.

Disambiguation

Waiting around a corner
catacorner in a square
of afternoon, looking like
nothing and without
warning is the
feeling—stalking you.

It is what makes you
follow shadows of adjacent
conversations and lick
the film from every
exchange, that first forming
hate, the taste of its food

It waits, smoking
the veins, and you wait too,
like something on a corner
organizing coincidence,
fixing the shock of its smell.

It lurks as circumspection,
extra sweaters, open
to generous
interpretation.

And you lurk too,
like a rain-faded can
in the light wind of youth

Oh but sometimes you see it
in the suicide light
of the moon

And that is its terror:

its pure arbitrary body,
its sheer hormonal skill.

Only Something

Only something with no
need—
warped by element, loved
into recession

Only something with no
mother, a boat on its water,
afloat and nowhere

could refuse the harbor

Something with no vacancy,
no hunger, cropping its own
low capacity

No birth wound, no age ring,
something strayed
by spontanaeity

Only something with primal
border, with mineral
armor

could turn from this offering

Like a peak you sometimes
see, not a chain of anything

Seasonal Poem

Snow would be the right weather
for today. Whiteness indicating
things that don't exist. And a numbness
and a blanketing to recollect mother

Its second stage is frozenness, and though I long
for its touch across my face, its coldness
settling, what seems to happen
quicker than it should is the snow's
paralysis. How willing it is
to take on other substances. How I used to run
to it barefoot before I thought
of my own comfort.

But the fall for which we've wished
the year is reticent; it hates its unreal
status, its intermittentness.

I could take a job—I've been thinking
about my purposes—collecting ice
for the eyes of the princess

Changing Contours

I cannot say it in any nice
way: I hate to see you
nowadays. My friends are not
nice: one of them said
you had aged twenty years;
and I am not nice: I swelled
with pride; another one said
you looked severe. He said
you gave him a crushing grip;
he had to pack his hand in ice.

I remember I left my useless
map on the wall; do you still
look at it? It showed the world
before it broke up into separate
continents.

Stunted Things, a Miscellany

one:
Feeling for the bonsai we
move among the installation
a little guilty.

Rocks below our feet
remind us of adversity.

Inherent in dwarfed
branches, twisted bark—
age—an unavoidable quality,
which in these trees,

trained to coil beachwood,
displays futility. We wonder
which we'd choose—death
or deformity.

Each specimen, though
the tableau, resists
the center. We wonder
which we'd choose—perfection
or humility.

We move outdoors
where the regular trees
normalize us. I myself do not feel

relieved. Indelibly, for weeks,
the lightest step, most imperceptible
breeze, a diminishing.

Roman Tone

What is the right way
to describe the want
to stand by—a pocket
of uncomprehending sound,
reprieve in sweltering
    significance

The desire to stick
like the under pitch
above which the fast
talk swarms

It isn't caution.
In fact some see
a recklessness
in the drive to be—
not a roadblock
but a thing in the road
redolent of dead
    animal

I'm not hurting anyone—
my passion for patch
of sand, unheeding
heart turned low

THE SOUND OF THE CLOSING DOOR

There is a kind of cry at first,
not of pain but of warning
of pain.

I have come to regard the wide arms
of the chair as an only mother.

Next a small suck of air.

I think my double is
the stone—fire-wrought or dripped
into formation. And there was
a third kind too.

Then two dry clicks, an interlocking.

It seems that it should be my lot
to look out on a line strung
from post to post,
and though it could be missed,
the dusk reminder of the small
daily apocalypse.

It is this third kind I relate to.

The first fragment of division,
the private room.

Neglect

The life that was
waiting for me is
gone. It was
there so long I'd
thought it was
part of me.

It used to hover
at the skin of me
or farther off
like a boy
I once kept
not too far,
close

enough to be
a motion I thought
my own.

It didn't happen
suddenly
or in dark.
In truth it went
patiently
like someone
packing from a list,
planning to
go thoroughly

In truth it went
slow.

I think of it now
but without it
it's like a privacy
emptied-out, a thought
closed.

It's not that: I've been
left before. It's like
when I was young,
what I thought
music was.

Once it loved nothing
but to wait for me

and I thought it
somewhere I could go.
Thought I could walk
into it when I was
done, like

entering a building
whose objects come
from home,
just enough

like my life that I'd
go, and at the back
not a light but
a source.

In a certain way,
nothing's much
changed. It's like
not knowing to count
and then counting
to one.

Belated thanks to my teachers Richard Howard, Marie Ponsot, and Bill Knott. Posthumous thanks to DHL for thought-variants on constraint. Bottomless thanks to Brian Hoffman and Alexander Stille for generosity without measure.

Gratitude to the following journals for publishing some of these poems in their pages: *American Poetry Review*; *Boston Review*; *Columbia: A Journal of Literature & Art*; *LATR*; *Open City*; *Passages North*; *Small Spiral Notebook*; *Verse*. Thanks also to *The Swallow Anthology of New American Poets*, in which four poems from this volume appeared.

Priscilla Becker's first book of poems, *Internal West*, won *The Paris Review* Book Prize, and was published in 2003. Her poems have appeared in *American Poetry Review, Boston Review, Fence, Open City, The Paris Review, Raritan, Small Spiral Notebook, Verse*, and *The Swallow Anthology of New American Poets*; her music reviews in *The Nation* and *Filter*; her book reviews in *The New York Sun*; and her essays in *Cabinet* magazine and *Open City*. Her essays have also been anthologized by Anchor Books, Sarabande, and Soft Skull Press. She teaches poetry at Pratt Institute, Columbia University, and in her apartment.